Revolution and Romanticism, 1789-1834
A series of facsimile reprints chosen and introduced by
Jonathan Wordsworth
University Lecturer in Romantic Studies at Oxford

Frend
Peace and union 1793

William Frend

Peace and union
1793

Woodstock Books
Oxford and New York
1991

This edition first published 1991 by
Woodstock Books
Spelsbury House, Spelsbury, Oxford OX7 3JR
and
Woodstock Books
Wordsworth Trust America
Department of English, City College
Convent Ave and 138th St, New York, N.Y. 10031

British Library Cataloguing in Publication Data
Frend, W. H. C. (William Hugh Clifford)
  Peace and union: 1793. – (Revolution and romanticism,
  1789-1834)
  1. Great Britain. Social reform, history
  I. Title   II. Series
  303.484
  ISBN 1-85477-066-7

Printed and bound in Great Britain by
Smith Settle
Otley, West Yorkshire LS21 3JP

Introduction

'At this moment perhaps the decree is gone forth for war'
– William Frend, Unitarian minister and Fellow of Jesus
College, Cambridge, was writing the final paragraph of
Peace and union in the last days of January 1793. Louis
XVI (styled by the French and their sympathisers, Louis
Capet, since the declaration of the Republic in
September) had been executed on the 21st; France would
declare war on 1 February, and England follow suit on
the 11th. There can seldom have been less prospect of
harmony and union between the British groups of
republicans and anti-republicans to whom Frend adressed
himself. Rumours of 'civil commotions' had led in
December to the calling out of local militias and the recall
of Parliament. In the Commons on 13 December, and
again in his published *Letter* to the Westminster Electors,
the Whig leader, Charles James Fox, had warned against
over-reaction:

Those who differ from us in their ideas of the constitution, in
this paroxysm of alarm we consider as confederated to destroy
it.

Frend's is a case in point. Though his brief appendices,
'On the Execution of Louis Capet' and 'The Effect of War
on the Poor', were more contentious, he made in *Peace
and union* a sincere attempt to reason the extremes of
British politics towards a middle ground. As a result he
was publicly tried by the University and deprived of his
Fellowship. 'Were not the times', the Vice Chancellor
demanded in his closing speech,

most critical? Did the author inculcate the necessity of peace and
good order? When the national convention of France had filled
up the measure of their crimes, by murdering the king, and
destroying all lawful government, and their deliberations
breathed nothing but atheism and anarchy, did he inculcate a
respect for the king and parliament of this country, and for the
reformed religion, and the functions of the clergy as established
by law?

About the functions of the clergy, Frend, as a Unitarian, had strong views – 'The established church of England can be considered only as a political institution', 'There are few congregations which worship only the one true god' – but even in this area he is seldom provocative. In general, he does indeed 'inculcate the necessity for peace and good order'. It is his primary concern.

Frend's view, stated at the outset of *Peace and union*, is that 'the utmost vigour of government, aided by the exertions of every lover of his country, is necessary to preserve us from all the horrours attendant on civil commotions.' The situation in France he sees as 'an awful example, which providence holds out to an astonished world'. The September Massacres have been shocking, but so was the misery that existed under the *ancien régime*. It must be possible to learn from both:

The assassinations, murders, massacres, burning of houses, plundering of property, open violations of justice, which have marked the progress of the French revolution, must stagger the boldest republican in his wishes to overthrow any constitution: and on the other hand he must be a weak or a wicked man, who lost in admiration of the beauties of a voluptuous and effeminate court, forgets the misery of the poor subjects, whose bodies were bowed down to the grindstone for its support, and brands with every mark of aristocratick insolence the efforts of those patriots, who put an end to the despotism of the antient government.

The original readers of Frend's pamphlet would have seen him as steering a path between the 'aristocratick insolence' of Burke and the 'bold republicanism' of Paine (now a French deputy, but condemned by a British court for seditious libel on 18 December).

Frend is a reformer, by most standards a moderate. The lesson to be learned from France is above all of failure to act in time:

From neglecting to examine and correct the abuses, prevailing through length of time in an extensive empire, we have seen a monarch hurled from his throne, the most powerful nobility in Europe driven from their castles, and the richest [clerical] hierarchy expelled from their altars.

The different orders of French society, even the affluent priesthood, could all have survived had they accepted the need to modify existing institutions:

> Had the monarch seasonably given up some useless prerogatives, he might still have worn the crown; had the nobility consented to relinquish those feudal privileges, which were designed only for barbarous ages, they might have retained their titles; could the clergy have submitted to be citizens, they might still have been in possession of wealth and influence.

'The proper time', Frend adds, 'to correct any abuse, and remedy any grievance, is the instant, they are known'.

From an English point of view, the words contained a threat. Was it already too late to examine peaceably 'the abuses, prevailing through length of time in [Britain's] extensive empire'? Frend does not think so. He has practical, humanitarian suggestions to put forward for modifying the constitution, increasing representation (so that 'all laws relating to the conduct of an individual would not only be known to him, but receive his approbation or censure'), assisting the not-quite-so-poor (the class that is Wordsworth's concern in *The last of the flock*), disestablishing the Church: what could prevent George III (who, as King of England and Scotland and Elector of Hanover, is a member of three different churches himself) from saying to all, 'Be peaceable citizens, and worship god as you please'? Anxious as he is for peace, Frend is not without a sharp side to his tongue. Representation is to exclude those 'obstinately attached to vicious and bad customs'; the priest, 'whether he celebrates the orgies of Bacchus, or solemnizes the rites of the Eucharist', will oppose every truth that threatens his authority; to secure the repeal of the Test Act, presbyterians, baptists and independents might band together, but they

> would on the obtaining of that point, retire to their different camps, and be separated from each other by the usual marks of theological hatred.

Frend had been an Anglican parson himself until, learning Hebrew and becoming a translator of the bible (his work was burned by the mob that destroyed Priestley's house in July 1791), he decided that scriptural evidence was against the doctrine of the Trinity. Conversion to Unitarianism in 1787 cut him off both from the 'men in black' of the established Church (he alone wore blue in the Common Room at Jesus) and from dissenters who believed 'idolatrously' in the divinity of Christ. As he made clear at the trial, however, his creed is love:

if we neglect the principle of universal benevolence, our faith is vain, our religion is an empty parade of useless and insignificant sounds . . . every christian is bound to entertain sentiments of universal benevolence, to love his fellow creatures of every sect, colour or description . . .

Coleridge, who was a member of Frend's college, and by this stage a disciple, applauded him so vigorously from the gallery that he barely escaped arrest by the Proctor. Intellectually Coleridge's Unitarianism of the mid 1790s derives from Priestley (and Hartley). But it was Frend's more emotional faith that inspired his vision of 'the vast family of Love / Rais'd from the common earth by common toil' (*Religious musings*). It also supported for a time the hopes he placed in a smaller, emigrant 'family of love' (Pantisocracy) on the banks of the Susquehanna.

The change of tone as Frend brings *Peace and union* to an end and moves into his appendices could hardly be more abrupt. One moment we are reading a plea that 'republicans be moderate in their demands, the anti-republicans not pertinacious in opposing every reform', the next we hear that 'Louis Capet has provided an excellent topic for parliamentary declamation':

The supreme power in the nation declared, that France should be a republick: from that moment Louis Capet lost his titles. He was accused of enormous crimes, confined as a state prisoner, tried by the national convention, found guilty, condemned, and executed. What is there wonderful in all this? . . . If Louis Capet did, when king, encourage the invasion of his country, however we may be inclined to pity the unfortunate man for the errour of his conduct, we have no right to proclaim him innocent in point of law.

'It is in short no business of ours', Frend adds, 'and if all the crowned heads on the continent are taken off, it is no business of ours.' Perhaps it was a little provocative.

Like the Wordsworth whose *Letter to the bishop of Llandaff* (February 1793) dismisses mourning for Louis as an 'idle cry of modish lamentation', Frend reserves his sympathy for the poor who will suffer especially from the war that is starting. Walking from Cambridge to St Ives to see his pamphlet through the press, he overhears the conversation of market-women who have had their wages for spinning wool reduced by a quarter: 'We are to be sconced three-pence in the shilling . . . We are to be sconced a fourth part of our Labour. What is all this for?' In Wordsworth's phrase, the women and their families are 'about to smart under the scourge of labour, of cold, and of hunger', in 'a war from which not a single ray of consolation can visit them'. It is from their uncomprehending complaints that Frend creates his vehement concluding paragraph:

At this moment perhaps the decree is gone forth for war. Let others talk of glory, let others celebrate the heroes, who are to deluge the world with blood, the words of the poor market women will still resound in my ears, we are sconced three-pence in the shilling, one fourth of our labour. For what!

J W

PEACE AND UNION

RECOMMENDED TO

THE ASSOCIATED BODIES OF

REPUBLICANS

AND

ANTI-REPUBLICANS;

By WILLIAM FREND, M. A.

FELLOW OF JESUS COLLEGE, CAMBRIDGE.

Printed for the AUTHOR,

BY P. C. CROFT, ST. IVES 1793.

(PRICE ONE SHILLING)

PEACE and UNION.

THE royal proclamations and the number of associated bodies on various pretexts in different parts of the kingdom are a sufficient proof, that the minds of men are at present greatly agitated; and that the utmost vigour of government, aided by the exertions of every lover of his country, is necessary to preserve us, from falling into all the horrours attendant on civil commotions. Having been warned of our danger, it becomes us to consider, by what means we may escape the impending evil: and no one should take a decisive part, without weighing fully and impartially the consequences of his conduct. The assassinations, murders, massacres, burning of houses, plundering of property, open violations of justice, which have marked the progress of the French revolution, must stagger the boldest republican in his wishes to overthrow any constitution: and on the other hand he must be a weak or a wicked man, who lost in admiration of the beauties of a voluptuous and effeminate court, forgets the miseries of the poor subjects, whose bodies were bowed down to the grindstone for its support, and brands with every mark of aristocratick insolence the efforts of those patriots, who put an end to the despotism of the antient

government

government. It is an aweful example, which providence holds out to an aftonifhed world; and happy will that nation be, which derives from it leffons of wifdom. Surely there cannot be a diffentient voice on this opinion; and no blame can that writer incur, who calls on the contending parties in our own country, to make a proper ufe of the divine judgements, and inftead of exafperating each other by ufelefs invectives, to unite cordially in their endeavours to promote the common good, and to remove thofe grievances, if any fuch there be, which occafion the prefent difcontent.

If the difpute between the contending parties were folely this, whether the prefent government fhould be overthrown or not, the matter might be brought to a fpeedy iffue. It would be urged on the one fide, that the government has for thefe hundred years laft paft been acknowledged as the beft in Europe, and unlefs a much better is pointed out to us, it will be unwife in the extreme to deftroy a fyftem, under which we have experienced fo much publick and private happinefs. The advocates for a republick may anfwer, that the government among many bad ones was really the beft, but the expences of it were enormous, a thoufand millions of money have been drawn from the fubjects, which, had they been expended on the country, would have converted it

into

into a paradife, and we have now before us the inftances of America and France, which on the ruins of their antient forms have erected much nobler edifices. Let us fee, whether a reafonable and moderate man may not be able to bring thefe parties nearer to each other. The governments of the reft of Europe are in general fuppofed by all Englifhmen to be much worfe than their own. In common with them ours took its origin from the feudal fyftem, but from a variety of caufes moft of the evils attendant on that fyftem, which retained their force on the continent have been, in our country gradually abolifhed; that the expences of government have been enormous muft be confeffed by all parties, but this is not fo much owing to the form of our conftitution, as to the wretched plan, introduced in the laft century, of anticipating in one the revenues of the fucceeding years. Let us caft a veil over this failing of our common anceftours, and endeavour, that pofterity fhall have no reafon to reproach us, for following with open eyes fo fhameful an example. The prefent fituation of France forbids us, to confider as yet its conftitution as worthy of imitation. It has not received the fanction of experience, and we muft wait till the wretched defpots, who with unparalleld infolence dared to interrupt its courfe, confent to leave a nation in poffeffion of the undoubted
right

right to form its own internal government.
Much lefs can America be urged as an example
for us: our cuftoms, laws and fituation have in-
ured us to habits unknown to the new world,
and a fudden change from our form to theirs
might be as prejudicial to the happinefs of this
country, as the impofition of our conftitution
might be to the inhabitants of America. Befides,
if inftead of the conftitutions of France and
America the moft perfect fyftem, that human
ingenuity can devife, fhould be prefented to us,
it does by no means follow, that we fhould be
juftifiable in forcing the acceptance of it on our
fellow countrymen. Every change is attended
with danger, and none fhould be adopted, where
the individuals injured by it are very numerous
in proportion to thofe, who are benefited.
The happinefs of this generation is to be taken
in to the eftimate, and it is not fufficient to affure
us, that the profpects of a future race will be im-
proved by our fchemes. Where is the man,
who can look fo far forward into futurity, as to
convince us, that our fucceffours might not fron
a different concatenation of circumftances receive
far greater bleffings, than we can beftow on them
by the ruin of ourfelves. As therefore the overthrow of our conftitution, with or without the
introduction of the moft perfect fyftem, could not
be compaffed without injuring a vaft number of
                                                  our

our fellow creatures, it fhould feem, that the contending parties might accede nearer to each
other, if it could be proved, that our government
is fufceptible of improvement, and that various
changes might be introduced for the benefit of
the community at large, without injuring a fingle individual. If this fhould appear to be the
cafe, we may, confiftently with our duty to ourfelves and pofterity, take the proper fteps for meliorating our condition, and leave to future generations the care of bringing government to the
utmoft point of perfection.

There is no fubject, on which the contending
parties are fo much at variance, as on that of
parliamentary reform. On the one hand it is
afferted, that the conftitution, as fettled at the
revolution, muft remain inviolate; on the other,
that the corruptions of government render a
reform in the reprefentation of the people, and the
duration of parliaments abfolutely neceffary.
Reform is a very vague word, and it is too often
made either a term of reproach or commendation,
as it fuits the intereft of the fpeaker. The true
fenfe of the word implies, that the things to be
reformed had been previoufly in a better ftate;
and that the intention of the reformer is to bring
them to their original deftination. Let us then
divide our difputed topick into its two component
parts, a reform of the duration of parliaments, and

B   the

the reprefentation of the people, and confidering each feparately, fee whether we may not on fome points bring the contending parties to an agreement.

I. On the duration of Parliaments. One party is for fhortening this duration, and reducing it to a period, on which there is a variety of opinions, fome being for triennial, fome for biennial and others for annual parliaments. Here we find a common point of union, for the other contending party declares its attachment to the government founded at the revolution, in which triennial parliaments are a confiderable feature. We may fay then to the advocates for fhortening the duration of parliaments, agree that three years fhall be the period, and the other contending party muft, unlefs it hath loft every fentiment of propriety, concur with you in promoting fo falutary a meafure. If it doth not, the publick muft fee clearly, that its reverence for the conftitution founded at the revolution is merely a pretence, to gain over to its fide the favour of a deluded populace.

II. On a reform of the reprefentation of the people.

The moft clamorous perfon for this fpecies of reform, might be ftaggered with a fimple queftion. Have the people of England been ever fo well reprefented as at the prefent moment?

The

The number of votes in feveral boroughs has been confiderably diminifhed, in others much enlarged, fince the charters were firft given to them: but it is not improbable that the number on the whole has been increafed. In counties the qualification for a vote is a freehold worth forty fhillings a year; and if we reflect on the increafe of riches in this country within the laft hundred years, we cannot hefitate to affirm that the number of freeholders muft have been confiderably enlarged. If therefore the mere increafe of the number of voters were an object to one of our contending parties, we might tell them, that time was gradually removing their complaints: but a wife and temperate man would not give fuch an anfwer, when he confidered, that time was alfo increafing fome complaints, and that government is properly called on to rectify the abufes prevailing in feveral boroughs. In the courfe of not many years muft the electours of one place grapple in the waves for their town, and at prefent a feptennial confequence is given to a heap of ruins. This is a real evil, and ought to be redreffed, and it muft be redreffed, as foon as men turn from the clamorous loquacity of pretended oratours and politicians to the fober dictates of common fenfe. The fevereft farcafm againft the houfe of commons is to be found in the writings of a parliamentary declaimer, diftinguifhed

guifhed by his purfuits of reform even to the privacies of his fovereign and the remote corners of the eaft, while he remains a declared enemy to the word, when it comes home to himfelf and his own connections. " The houfe of commons, " fays this writer, is within itfelf a much more " fubtle and artful combination of parts and pow- " ers, than people are generally aware of. " What knits it to the other members of the " conftitution, what fits it to be at once the great " fupport and the great controul of government, " what makes it of fuch admirable fervice to " that monarchy, which, if it limits, it fecures " and ftrengthens, would require a long difcourfe " belonging to the leifure of a contemplative man " not to one, whofe duty it is to join in com- " municating practically to the people the bleff- " ings of fuch a conftitution." In other words by means of rotten boroughs men of fortune are able to raife a party againft, and to clog the wheels of government, by means of places and penfions government is enabled to oppofe them: the houfe is like a field of battle, with this dif- ference only, that the victorious party changes feats and opinions with the conquered, and the conteft is renewed.*

The

---

* If to deal out the moft virulent invectives againft perfons in poffeffion of power, if to coalefce with thofe very perfons to
gain

The fact then being undeniable, that feveral of our boroughs have grown worfe fince the revolution, we may fairly call on our contending parties to concur in rectifying this abufe. The evil might without much inconvenience be remedied by a plan fimilar to the one following. Let a lift be made out of the voters in every borough, and let it be ordered by parliament, that every borough, not having a thoufand voters, fhall out of the inhabitants of the town or hundred gradually raife them to that number. It is faid gradually, otherwife the new comers might be too infolent with their acquired power; and on that account the boroughs having five hundred voters fhould increafe their number by fifty every year, thofe under that number by twenty or thirty. Thus the boroughs will be brought gradually

C

nearer

gain a fhare of that power, if to draw down the tears and fhatter the nerves of fafhionable fenfibility, and overwhelm with opprobrious language a perfon, whofe power once extended over a vaft empire, if thefe are the marks of a great oratour and politician, the writer, whom I have quoted, carries away the palm from every hero in every age. Whether Mr. Haftings is guilty or not of the high crimes laid to his charge, I fhall not pretend to determine, and it appears to me, that very few indeed will be able to lay their hands on their breafts, and from a perufal of the evidence and fpeeches declare upon their honour, that he is either guilty or not guilty. The fpeeches of the celebrated declaimer above alluded to, muft from the nature of his language, have made a great impreffion on many minds in favour of the much injured governour.

nearer to their original form; but neither party muft imagine, that the mere increafe of voters will without other fteps fecure the integrity of the electours or the reprefentatives.

It is a trite remark that to a foreigner the people of England feem every feven years infected with madnefs. On the one hand are to be feen gentlemen of the firft rank ruining their eftates to ingratiate themfelves with the populace, on the other the people giving themfelves up to every fpecies of intemperance. This is an evil, which calls loudly for redrefs; and it would be well if the contending parties, confining themfelves folely to the rectifying of this abufe, would lay a foundation for the praifes and improvement of pofterity.

If vaft multitudes are permitted to be called together, and treated at the expence of the candidates, this evil will always remain; and the only way to remove it is by devifing fome plan, which fhall fecure to the electour an eafy way of giving his vote with as little infringement on his time as poffible. The practice of calling a county together on a day of nomination is attended with manifeft inconvenience. The county cannot be affembled, and the mode of determining the fenfe of fuch meetings is vague and inconclufive.

If

If there is any neceffity for a day of nomination, the advantages expected from it, might be
better fecured by delegates from parifhes fum-
moned by the fheriff of the county. Thus on
an appointed day let the freeholders meet in their
refpective parifhes, and every perfon being at
liberty to name a candidate, let them elect a delegate to carry the lift to the general meeting.
At this meeting let the delegates confer together
in the prefence of the fheriff, as prefident, on the
merits of the candidates, and having given their
votes let each take with him the refult, to be
laid before the freeholders on the day of election.
On that day the delegate being the prefident of
the parifh meeting fhould acquaint the electours
with what had paffed on the day of nomination,
and receiving their votes fhould make out two
lifts, the one to be carried to the fheriff, the
other to be preferved in the parifh. On a fub-
fequent day the delegates fhould again meet the
fheriff, who cafting up the numbers fhould declare thofe to be the reprefentatives, who had the
majority of votes in their favour. Thus members would be returned to parliament with very
little interruption to the induftry of the country,
and if we take into the eftimate the bribes, the
quarrels, the riots, the drunkennefs, the pro-
fanenefs, the blafphemies, the perjuries, which
will be avoided by this plan, no one who is a
friend

friend to religion or virtue can hefitate to give it his heartfelt concurrence.*

Our conftitution, admitting a reprefentative government, permits us to reafon on it, and fpeculative men will naturally be led to purfue their refearches on fuch a fubject to a greater degree of refinement, than is pleafing to the vulgar, to whom they feem to be trifling with utopian fchemes and imaginary ideas of perfection. Still men of thought fhould not be difcouraged by the vague furmifes of rude and uncultivated minds. Had the prefent conftitution of our country been propofed to the valiant band under William the conquerour, it would have been received as an impracticable fcheme, the wildeft that the brain of man had ever conceived, and the fchemes which we deride may be the means of innumerable bleffings to future generations. Let the fpeculative man then indulge himfelf in his theories; and let us propofe to him to enquire, whether reprefentative government can be carried on to perfection, on a better plan than that laid down by an infpired legiflatour, and adopted in

part

---

* The term freeholder has been ufed, but there feems to be no reafon, why the copyholders fhould be excluded from the right of fuffrage. And inftead of requiring a certain qualification in landed property from the candidate, any man who had a majority of votes fhould take his feat in the houfe and be allowed for obvious reafons five hundred a year for his attendance.

part by the wifeft monarch, that ever fat on the
Englifh throne.

The divifions of hundreds and tithings being
adopted, let the perfons of age in each tithing
elect a prefident, let the prefidents of ten tithings
elect the prefident of the hundred, the prefidents
of ten hundreds elect the prefident of the thoufand and fo on. Each divifion of ten thoufand
families fhould fend two members to parliament.
The voters fhould be taken by the heads of tithings, and carried by them to the heads of hundreds,
to be conveyed to the heads of thoufands, who
with the head of the ten thoufand fhould declare
the reprefentatives elected. Thus none but the
officers would be put to any material inconvenience in giving their votes : the offices fhould be
annual and biennial, the headfhips of tithings
and hundreds annual, the reft biennial.

Such a divifion would not only be ufeful for
the purpofes of obtaining a better reprefentation
in parliament, but it might likewife reftore the
peace and tranquillity, which is faid to have pre-
vailed in the days of Alfred. Thus the prefidents
of hundreds and the fuperiour divifions might be
invefted with the power of a juftice of the peace,
an officer of the greateft publick utility, very
much wanted at prefent in many extenfive diftricts. From the prefidents of hundreds the
grand jury fhould always be felected, and the

D   petty

petty jury from the heads of tithings. All laws that have received the fanction of parliament fhould be fent to the prefidents of ten thoufands, by them to be diftributed among the inferiour divifions, fo that every law relating to the people in general fhould be fent to the heads of tithings, particular bills to the heads of hundreds and the fuperiour divifions. The laws received by the head of a tithing fhould be read to the tithing, and if objected to by the majority, the objection with the number of votes fhould be fent to the head of the hundred, and by him to the fuperiour officer and fo on; and if it fhould appear that the majority of the kingdom was againft any bill, it fhould be fubjected to a revifion in the next parliament. Thus would two main points be gained by this divifion of the country; the houfe of commons would, as far as human imperfection admits, be really a reprefentation of the people, and all laws relating to the conduct of an individual would not only be known to him, but receive his approbation or cenfure.

We fhould pay too great a compliment to our countrymen by fuppofing them capable of receiving or acting under fo enlarged a plan of reprefentation. The minds of men muft be more enlightened, the lower claffes muft be better inftructed, a more familiar and friendly intercourfe

muft

muſt take place between all ranks of ſociety, before ſuch a plan could produce its due effect.

This conſideration ought to have ſome weight with the contending parties. The one might be ſpurred on to teach the lower claſſes by every mean in their power the bleſſings of a free and good government, and the ardour of the other for introducing new forms might, by reflecting on the real ſtate of the peaſantry of this country, be conſiderably repreſſed. And, by accuſtoming ourſelves to reflect on the difficulties on both ſides of the queſtion, we might all with better temper liſten to the remarks made on government by men of oppoſite parties; we ſhould not confound republicans with levellers, and to the exaggerating encomiaſters of the preſent conſtitution with all its defects, we might apply the words of eaſtern wiſdom, Let another man praiſe thee, and not thine own mouth, a ſtranger and not thine own lips.*

To hear ſome perſons talk of perfect repreſentation, one would imagine that it muſt be the precurſour of a ſecond golden age. The wiſdom of the nation would be collected as it were into a focus, but we forget that its folly would be as forcibly concentrated. If the majority of a nation conſiſts of weak, ignorant, and barbarous

D 2 characters

* Prov. xxvii. 2.

characters, incapable of being meliorated by religion, and obstinately attached to vicious and bad customs, it cannot be suppofed that their reprefentatives fhould excell in virtue, or that the laws compofed by them fhould be calculated for general happinefs. If the people were fuperftitioufly inclined, perfecution againft individuals of a different opinion would receive the fanction of their houfe of commons with the fame eafe, as it has been enforced by the edicts of a defpotick prince: and the lover of peace and tranquillity, the philofopher whofe refearches extend our knowledge, and the cultivatour of the arts, which foften and embellifh life, would feek for that liberty under the fhade of an arbitrary court, which was denied to them by the laws or conduct of a tumultuous rabble.††

Hence then let us ferioufly recommend to the contending parties to employ their thoughts on other topicks befide thofe of parliamentary reform, left being attached to a fingle object, they overlook the abufes, which may gradually undermine the peace and happinefs of fociety. Some of the affociated bodies have very properly declared, that our conftitution has provided the

means

†† Zimmerman relates fomewhere in his excellent work on folitude an anecdote of a gentleman who wifhed to enjoy the liberty of fpeaking his fentiments on all fubjects. For this purpofe he chofe Zurich, ftaid there ten days, and then retired to Lifbon.

means of rectifying abuses, and they would do well to point out thofe which require immediate reform. We may celebrate in the loudeft tone the praifes of our conftitution, yet if our laws are vague and inconciufive, eafily to be wrefted by the powerful, and too expenfive for the poor, if punifhments bear no proportion to crimes, and the moft atrocious murderer is levelled with a petty delinquent, it muft be confeffed that a ftranger would have reafon to exclaim, the theory of your government is excellent, but your laws betray a degree of rudenefs and barbarity not to be expected in fo enlightened a nation.

Our laws ftand certainly in need of reform, and it were to be wifhed that the leading powers in our fenate would exert themfelves in giving us a better code. The evil is acknowledged by all parties, but it is the fuppofed intereft of one to increafe by voluminous digefts the intricacy of the law. It might be urged that the laws affecting the lower claffes of the people fhould be equal, clear, and decifive, fuch that a fchool-boy might read them, and be brought up with a fenfe of their propriety, and a fear of offending them. This without doubt would be of great advantage to the poor; and the political writers of the laft century recommended the practice of a neighbouring country, by which the rich might be equally benefited. Many of them are to their

coft

eoft acquainted with the expenfivenefs of fuits depending on the litigation of landed property, which would be at an end by the eafy plan of regiftering it in every county. Some perfons complain, that they have found a difficulty of recovering, or have even loft an eftate from the imperfect regifters of births in parifhes, from which all that are not members of the church are excluded. Suppofing a civil arrangement for thefe purpofes, the land of every perfon and the births of all children might be fo regiftered, as to prevent a multiplicity of law fuits. A fiction in law is a mean at prefent of faving the country from the iniquity and oppreffion attending the abfurd and barbarous cuftom of retailing property on remote defcendants, but would it not be much better by acting in an open and direct manner to prevent the father from forgetting the ties of blood, and by abolifhing entails entirely oblige every one to act up to the principles of juftice. Manerial rights were of ufe in the feudal ages, but different times produce different cuftoms, and a revifal of all the laws in manours might be made beneficial to the lord and his dependant. Our game laws are cruel and oppreffive, contrary to every principle of good government, and calculated only to produce a fpirit of ariftocratick infolence in the higher, and that of meannefs, pilfering, and plunder in the loweft

claffes

claffes. It has been urged in their defence, that if it were not for them, we fhould be overrun with poachers; but in fact, as high duties made the fmugglers, the game laws make the poachers. Deftroy the game laws entirely, let game be fold freely in our markets, and the poachers, as the fmugglers have done lately in many places, will return to the habits of ufeful induftry. We muft not omit here, that the higher claffes will be benefited: for in what county can we go without hearing of the petty fquabbles of country fquires, about hares and partridges, naufeous tales, difgufting to every man of fenfe and a liberal education.

The amendment of the poor laws requires a cautious and fkillfull hand, and much praife is due to fome very refpectable members of the houfe of commons, for endeavouring to excite the attention of their colleagues to this fubject. There is an excellent precept in the mofaical law, which fhould be a guide to all legiflatours; thou fhalt not muzzle the ox which treadeth out the corn. The poor are the inftruments of the eafe, comfort, and luxury of the rich, and it would be contrary to the temper of englifhmen as well as the fpirit of chriftians to be ungrateful to thofe, from whom we all derive our fupport. If a labouring man does not receive fufficient wages to enable him to bring up a numerous family, and

to

to lay by fomething for his fupport in the decline of life, it is but common juftice, that they, who have been enriched by his labours, fhould, when his ftrength is gone, make his latter days chearful and comfortable. So far then from diminifhing the poor rates, there feems, unlefs the price of labour fhould be confiderably increafed, fufficient reafon for increafing them. The poor rates muft, if the price of labour is given, increafe with the increafe of taxes; for every tax laid on the confumption of the poor is a great diminution of his pittance, and the halfpenny or farthing, a trifle to the tax impofers, is feverely felt in the cottages of induftry. Should thefe laws be ever revifed, there is a clafs in fociety which may be greatly benefited; this is the clafs juft above poverty, juft above want themfelves, but by means of rates reduced to a worfe fituation, than thofe who receive their benefactions. To follow the beautiful gradations of nature in all her operations, this clafs fhould be releafed from the poor rates: thus there would be three claffes in fociety, that which pays to the relief of others, that which receives, and that which neither pays nor receives. A revifion alfo cannot take place without relieving the poor from the reftraints under which they at prefent labour in removing from one parifh to another, and the expenfivenefs of litigation arifing from the prefent code might perhaps be
remedied,

remedied. But in thefe affairs we muft, as was before mentioned, be particularly careful, left the poor fhould be injured: the rich can take care of themfelves, the poor have none to defend them, and the fault of moft governments feems chiefly to confift in this, that they pay the moft attention to the maintenance and fupport of the corinthian capitals of focicty, as fome orders have been foolifhly called, to the great neglect of the comfort and wellfare of the moft numerous and important part of the community.

The practice of the law at prefent, an evil, which time is likely to increafe, threatens to render the profeffion unworthy of a man of liberal education. To fet a young perfon down to copy declarations, pleas, replications, rejoinders, furrejoinders, rebutters, furrebutters, is not a probable mean of correcting his judgement, enlivening his imagination, or qualifying him to convince by the ardour of his eloquence. Yet it now feems neceffary that Demofthenes and Cicero fhould give place to the precedents in the office of a fpecial pleader: and, if our laws continue to increafe with the fame rapidity as they have done in the prefent reign, the future generation of barrifters muft fink into the level of vulgar mechanicks. Already we have feen the inferiority of the bar, when the beft fpecimens of its rhetorick were compared with the genuine

effufions

effufions of eloquence from our popular fpeakers.
The oratours of antient times, we are informed,
did not blufh to receive information from the
erudite profeffours of the law, and if the encou-
ragement of eloquence were thought of fufficient
importance, a fimilar arrangement of offices might
not be without its ufe. Were the attornies confined to their prefent employment: were fpecial
pleaders, men of cool heads and fit for fedentary
lives, occupied in arranging, explaining, digefting
our ftatutes and acts of parliament, were it their
bufinefs to take an action from the attorney's
hands, decide on its legality, and put it into due
form, to be prefented with every ftatute or cafe
relating to it to the barrifter, the time of this
latter character, the higheft in the profeffion,
might be employed in the purfuit of every fpecies
of liberal knowledge. It would not be expected
from him, to have an antiquarian infight into our
laws and cuftoms, nor to enter into all the detail
of an attorney's clerk; but we fhould look for ele-
gance of language, propriety of expreffion, con-
vincing eloquence, happy allufions, and to fum
up the whole in a few words, we fhould expect
to find in him both at the bar and at the table the
gentleman and the fcholar.*

* Since the inns of court have ceafed to be places of education, and the exercifes there are merely formal, might not the
priviledge of pleading at the bar be allowed to any one, in
whom the plaintiff places confidence.

The tedioufnefs of the law, as well as its un-
certainty, has been a frequent fubject of complaint; but, though deprecated by every one,
there does not feem any difpofition at prefent in
the lords or commons to probe thefe evils to the
bottom. Its language too is barbarous and rude:
for, under the pretence of avoiding by infinite
circumlocutions cavil and difpute, fcarce an act
of our legiflature is intelligible to a man of tole-
rable capacity; and the jargon of a profeffion,
which ought to ufe the cleareft and beft terms,
is now become proverbial. We fhould therefore be much indebted to the contending parties,
if they would unite their efforts in making an effectual reform in that part of our fyftem, on
which life, property, and reputation fo much
depend. The tafk is not fo arduous, as may be
apprehended: there are among us men of learning and abilities, as well qualified for this under-
taking as the celebrated lawyers in the days of
Juftinian; and the only thing required on the
part of the legiflature and people is to be ferioufly
perfuaded, that internal good government is more
productive of general happinefs, than the interference in foreign politicks and the triumphs of
a victorious navy.

In perufing the hiftory of antient or modern
times the connection, which has always taken
place between religion and legiflation muft ftrike

every

every attentive reader. This union is fuppofed to be of a peculiar nature, and while in our own country the grave divine celebrates it as an alliance between church and ftate, the jolly toper no lefs religioufly fills up the bumper to church and king. The latter character means no difrefpect to his fovereign, by making him give place to an inftitution efteemed facred by the vulgar; but the former, lamenting the lofs of ancient fplendour, is willing to retain as long as poffible this laft veftige of ecclefiaftical power. Seventeen centuries ago the church, creeping on the ground, bowed its head to the authority of Cæfar, within three centuries after we find her in the embraces of a warlike emperour; the harlot foon learned to tread on the necks of kings, and, drenched with the blood of faints and martyrs, obtained univerfal empire. Our anceftours groaned under her iron yoke, the fruit of their induftry was carried away to feed her pampered appetite, and to fatiate her luxurious paramours. The ifland was completely devoted to her luft; but vice is never fecure in its feat, it has no ftable hold, the fame capricious and inordinate paffions, which tempt men to forfake the fair object of their betrothed love, lead them foon to caft away in difguft the loathfome proftitute. To capricious and inordinate paffion we are indebted for deliverance from the harlots power: fhe can no longer free

the

the subject from his allegiance, nor compell the
monarch to accept the crown at the footstool of
her throne. Her superiority is gone, and protestant divines should beware of applying those
terms to a political institution of this country,
which must involve them in all the guilt of anti-
christian usurpation.

The alliance between church and state is a
fiction, which could not be realized in this country, without subjecting the abettours of it to the
penalties of high treason. We might as well
talk of an alliance between army and state, navy
and state, law and state. Would queen Elizabeth
have permitted this language, and is it not
equally certain, that such expressions must be
displeasing to every branch of the Brunswick
family? Has the state, from the moment it became
protestant, ever made an alliance with any church,
and do not all our ecclesiastical laws depend on
the authority of parliament? Where does the
church meet, where does it make laws, where
does it propose terms of mutual kindness to her
ally the state? In this island are two institutions
called the churches of England and Scotland, for
which the clergy of the church of England are
ordered by law to command the prayers of every
congregation. Are they both allies of the state?
Is there also any alliance between the two sacred
bodies? Let us beware of the deception couched
in

in ambiguous terms; for there is no fociety in this country, that can pretend to make terms with the ftate, nor is there any perfon, whofe authority does not depend on an act of parliament. And let divines be particularly cautious, left king and people, recollecting the fufferings of former times, fhould be tempted to fufpect, that, as long as there are priefts, the laity is in danger of being duped by the priefthood.

The eftablifhed church of England can be confidered only as a political inftitution. The defign of it is to celebrate at certain times religious worfhip, and to inftruct the people in certain doctrines laid down by act of parliament. Whether the inftruction communicated is fuited to the prefent times, and whether the expence attending it is proportioned to the benefits, which the fubject derives from it, are queftions of political enquiry. The farmer and the land-holder complain, that tithes are a grievous oppreffion, that thereby induftry is cramped, and our lands are deprived of their proper culture. Divines, fay they, laid a claim in former ages to the produce of our fields, in confequence of a regulation for very different purpofes in a diftant region, and they not only perfuaded our legiflature to adopt it, but have exacted the odious tax in a manner unknown to the favoured people of god. The cuftoms of Judea are no rule for this country,

and

and confequently it is no argument againft our
prefent mode of paying the clergy, that we have
deviated widely from the mofaical inftitution.
We are interefted only in the enquiry, whether
a certain body of men fhould depend on government or the people for its fubfiftence, or by pof-
feffing a confiderable ftake in the landed property
be in a great meafure rendered independant of
both.   The queftion has on every fide its difficulties.   Suppofing the clergy to be like the
army or navy under the executive power, there
is a danger in our complicated form of government, left the regal part fhould abforb that of the
other two bodies.   For ten thoufand men in
black under the direction of an individual are a
far more formidable body, than ten thoufand
times that number in arms, and more likely to
produce the greateft injury to civil fociety.

If checks could be found to remedy the inconvenience attending the abfolute dependance of the
clergy on the crown, fuch a fyftem would be
found to poffefs great advantages : for, as the mi-
litary are fent only, where their prefence is neceffary, the religious corps would be difpofed in a
manner more beneficial to the kingdom.   We
fhould not fee them in groupes in fome towns
encouraging or rather being the patrons of every
fpecies of luxury, while extenfive diftricts are
entrufted to the care of a few curates : a regular
                                    difpofition

difposition of them might take place, which, from a proper attention to the learning and morals in the candidates for the office of publick inftruc- tours, would be attended with infinite benefit to the lower claffes of the community. Here then is a fubject, which might ufefully employ the thoughts of our contending parties. Let them en- deavour to remove the complaints of our land- holders, taking care at the fame time that fo large a body as the clergy fhould not be entrufted with any temporal power, and that the profeffion fhould poffefs fuch emoluments, as might render it a proper purfuit for men of liberal education.

Every thing in this world convinces us, that there is only one being in his own nature un- changeable. The inftitutions of man can fcarce be fuited to one generation, and the wifdom of government would in no inftance more eminently difplay itfelf, than by accomodating its laws to the improvement of knowledge in every age. The parliament, which appointed, and the people, which received the form of worfhip now in ufe, entertained very different notions from ours on religious fubjects. It could not be otherwife : for, by rejecting many articles in the creed of their anceftours, they entered into controverfies, which paved the way for future improvement. This was perceived in the next century, but unfortu- nately the ruling powers, by calling together

men

men or too difcordant opinions, and endeavouring
to reconcile parties feparated from each other by
a feries of mutual injuries, confirmed by this ex-
periment a truth, with which they ought to have
been acquainted, that the councils of divines of
different churches are never attended with fuc-
cefs. The liturgy of the church of England
is a compofition derived from the mafs book of
Rome, over which if it has in fome refpects a manifeft fuperiority, it is very far from that ftandard
of purity in its arrangement, language, or doctrine,
which is required from fuch compofitions. The
ableft writers in its defence acknowledge, that it
is fufceptible of improvement, but are fearful of
the danger attending every reform. We have
feen the caufe of failure in the laft century, and,
to avoid the fplitting on the fame rock, might
not the legiflature appoint commiffioners of its
own church to revife the book of prayers, and to
propofe a form better fuited to the prefent times ?
This fhould not however fuperfede the liturgy
in prefent ufe. There may be congregations attached to the common liturgy, whofe prejudices
fhould be humoured, and, inftead of forcing another on any one, the legiflature need only permit
the approved forms to be read in thofe churches,
where the people are willing to give them admif-
fion. Thus continual improvements might be
made in the form of worfhip, the more imperfect

F   liturgies

liturgies would gradually difappear, and in a few centuries perhaps the religious antipathies of the prefent days would ceafe to influence the conduct and embitter the lives of our pofterity.

The reform of our religious eftablifhment cannot, it is obvious, engage our attention without fome animadverfions on a controverfy, which has been lately carried on with a confiderable degree of animofity. To preferve the eftablifhment it was thought neceffary in the laft century, to require from every officer under the executive government a religious teft. Of courfe a degree of honour has been attached to the believers or pretended be-lievers of certain doctrines, and the diffentients have been involved in a correfponding portion of difgrace. In confidering this queftion, we are to look upon thefe bodies merely as political factions; for, did we refer to the book, which both parties are fuppofed to make the guide of all their actions and opinions, the queftion will not admit a mo-ments debate. By calling themfelves chriftians, they ought in every inftance to yield to our faviour's precepts and example, and there is not a propofition in Euclid clearer than this, that no body of chriftians is authorifed by the gofpel, to allure men to its party by civil emoluments, or on account of religious opinions to deprive them of civil advantages.

Is

Is then a teſt neceſſary to preſerve the political exiſtence of the church of England? We ſhall be able to anſwer this queſtion by conſidering the danger, that would immediately accrue from the removal of the teſt. In ſome of our manu-facturing towns diſſenters would ſhare with churchmen in municipal offices: a few and very few would exerciſe in counties the office of juſtice of the peace. The latter office depending on the crown, the moment there was an appearance of danger, it might be removed by ſtriking the diſaffected out of the commiſſion. Now, is it probable, that an inſtitution, whoſe influence, from its own wealth conſiderable, is ſupported by that of the nobility and the greater part of the landed intereſt of this country, could receive any injury from the admiſſion of a few perſons in municipal offices. The ſuppoſition is abſurd and the apprehenſion of danger muſt ariſe, from a ſuſpicion of the diſſenters receiving on the removal of the teſt a vaſt acceſſion of numbers, united together in a firm reſolution, to deſtroy the religious eſtabliſhment. But perſons, who reaſon in this manner, are not aware, that the diſſenters do not by any means form a compact body; and that the three powers, preſbyterians, baptiſts, and independants, allied together for one ſingle pur-poſe, would on the obtaining of that point, retire to their different camps, and be ſeparated from

each

each other by the ufual marks of theological hatred.

On what ground are we to expect an increafe of their numbers? The majority of the people, who do not look forward to any thing but the fruits of their induftry, will always go to that place of worfhip, which they think the beft: and, unlefs it can be proved, that the worfhip of the three bodies above-mentioned is far fuperiour to that of the church of England, they muft remain, as they have been for fome time, increafing only with the increafing population of the country.

Let any man then compare together coolly the worfhip of thefe different bodies. The object of worfhip, generally fpeaking, for there are few congregations which worfhip only the one true god, is the fame in all; fome ufing a prefcribed form, others what is called extempore prayer. The fuperiority on either fide depends fo much on the abilities of the fpeakers or readers, that, on confidering the rank of life from whence they are refpectively taken, and the advantages of education, which they enjoy, it will appear improbable, that the church of England fhould be inferiour to its opponents. The harmonious numbers of Watt's hymns, the commonly received book among the diffenters, may be fuppofed to give them a fuperiority in one part of the fervice over the church; but the pfalms of Sternhold and

Hopkins,

Hopkins, though deficient in metre, do not inculcate unscriptural doctrines, nor does their language, though simple and unadorned, ever sink into the lullabies of the lyrick poet. The sermons of the church of England, whether considered as specimens of eloquence, as treatises of moral philosophy or didactick theology, do not suffer on a comparison with those of the dissenting party: and there are few churches, which could bear such language or sentiments, as are too frequently uttered in several meetings. Hence the danger, apprehended from the mode of worship among the three bodies above-mentioned, seems to be chimerical, and government has by a sufficiently accurate survey been informed, that the number of opponents to the church establishment cannot occasion any ground of alarm: but perhaps neither government, nor churchmen, nor dissenters are aware of the increase of a body, already more numerous and better organized than the latter party, and which may in no length of time occasion a revolution in our ecclesiastical history.

Although no danger is to be apprehended from the removal of the test, government may very fairly demand; what advantages shall we derive by departing from our old laws and favouring the dissenters? The answer is obvious. By removing a reasonable cause of complaint from the

most

moft induftrious and peaceable of your fubjects, you preferve a fteadier attachment to the eftablifhed authority. There is fomething in the heart of man, which revolts at oppreffion; and to be beloved, you muft render yourfelves worthy of affection. The conduct of churchmen towards diffenters has been, and is difgraceful in the extreme: it is time to caft away the leaven of party fpirit, and to act as chriftians. By this, fays our faviour, fhall all men know that ye are my difciples, if ye love one another. Did the repeal of the teft act depend only on one part of the legiflature, it cannot be fuppofed, that the redrefs of the diffenters would be delayed a moment. For, how could the firft magiftrate deny that to a great part of the people, which, in different places acknowledging his authority, he claims for himfelf. Either he is a member of the church of England, or he is not. If he is a member of the church of England, by paffing into Scotland he becomes a diffenter, but is not on that account deprived of his office: another form of religion prevails in Hanover, but he retains his electorate. What could prevent him then from faying to the diffenters; As my temporal office is not in other countries affected by my religious opinions, neither fhall you fuffer any civil injuries for diffenting from the eftablifhment of England. Be peaceable citizens, and

worfhip

worſhip god as you pleaſe; your religion no where teaches you to diſobey your civil governours, except when they preſume to interfere in matters of conſcience.

It is much to be lamented, that, in treating on a ſubject relating to religious opinions, we cannot perſuade the profeſſours of chriſtianity, to abide by the commands of their common maſter: inſtead of which, not only the ſtateſman, but thoſe, who pride themſelves on being miniſters of the goſpel, ſet up in direct oppoſition to him maxims of worldly policy. The line of truth is direct and clear, the paths of errour are infinite. In the conflicts of paſſions and prejudice in a houſe of commons the ſtill voice of chriſtianity cannot always be heard; the ſtateſman is too apt to conſider it as a ſilly deviſed fable, well calculated to keep the people in order, and there are few willing to receive it in the only manner, which commands attention, as the direct word of god. Hence perhaps the diſſenters would do well, to leave the ſtate entirely to itſelf, content, as the early chriſtians were, to draw men to a purer form of worſhip, and to truſt to a change of opinion for entire relief from perſecution. The moſt improbable tales were in early times vented of the chriſtians; their meetings were burnt down, and their perſons were aſſaulted. Is it to be wondered at, that the ſame practices ſhould, by the enlightened infidel

infidel, the interefted churchman, and the ignorant populace be in our days both repeated and
applauded ? The fame paffions will every where
produce on certain minds the fame effect ; and
the prieft in every age, whether he celebrates the
orgies of Bacchus, or folemnizes the rites of the
Eucharift, will, fhould either his victims or his
allowance fail, oppofe in either cafe every truth,
which threatens to undermine his altars, or
weaken his facerdotal authority.

The church ftands certainly in need of reform,
the diffenters would do well to confider alfo,
whether they are not far, very far from the fum-
mit of chriftian perfection. The few of us dif-
perfed over England, who through fear and love
of the one true god, are obliged to feparate ourfelves from both parties, cannot but view with
concern, that, while they are fo much occupied
in a matter of fmall temporal importance, the
great truths of religion are neglected: and we
muft never let flip any opportunity of exciting
them to examine and improve their feparate
forms of worfhip and religious communion. That
chriftianity has made very little progrefs for the
laft fourteen hundred years, is obvious to every
reader of ecclefiaftical hiftory, and the profeffours
of it ought not to be furprized, fince, during fo
long a period, the world has been under the influence of two opinions, nearly fubverfive of all

true

true religion. The firſt is a very antient opinion, which it was the intention of the jewiſh diſpenſation to eradicate, by ſubſtituting in its place a long loſt and almoſt ſelf evident truth. That there is one god and only one god is ſuppoſed by many to be a truth attainable by human reaſon ; but if it were not ſo, the authority of revelation has eſtabliſhed it, and the whole heathen mythology is declared to be a fit object of ridicule.*
Still this truth, confirmed by various acts of omnipotence, did not overcome entirely the prejudices of the choſen people of god ; and as they aſſociated with the worſhip of Jehovah that of the neighbouring nations, the great body of chriſtians has imbibed, and glories in imbibing from the ſchools of Athens, opinions no where ſanctioned

G

oned

---

* A learned writer on the mythology of the ancients makes the following remarks on the groſſneſs of their ſuperſtition.

"Who would imagine, that one of the wiſeſt nations that "ever exiſted, could reſt ſatiſfied with ſuch idle figments : and "how can we account for theſe illuſions, which overſpread the "brighteſt minds? We ſee knowing and experienced people "inventing the moſt childiſh tales ; lovers of ſcience adopting "them ; and they are finally recorded by the grave hiſtorian : "all which would not appear credible, had not we theſe eviden-"ces ſo immediately tranſmitted from them. And it is to be "obſerved that this blindneſs is only in regard to their religion; "and to their mythology, which was grounded thereupon. In "all other reſpects they were the wiſeſt of the ſons of men." What will the writers on the mythology of the eighteenth century think a thouſand years hence of the european figments.

oned in fcripture, and has affociated the worfhip
of created beings, with that of the god and father of
Jefus Chrift. So great a deviation from truth
muft neceffarily be attempted with dreadful
effects, the moft folemn act of life is rendered
childifh, and the unbeliever confounding the purity of the gofpel with the prejudice of its
profeffours, thinks himfelf entitled to ridicule
religion, and to defpife chriftianity. Let churchmen and diffenters examine ferioufly how far they
have deviated from the true faith, and as they
reject many points eftablifhed by the councils of
the romifh church, let them expunge every thing,
which favouring of its leaven, is to be found in
prefbyterian fynods or epifcopal convocations.

When men blindly receive inftead of revealed
truths, the wild fancies of fpeculative heathens,
it is not to be wondered at, if the other parts of
their fyftem fhould be in oppofition to the plaineft
dictates of chriftianity. Our faviour was frequently under the neceffity of correcting the
foolifh vanity of his meffengers, and forefeeing
the evil confequences of ambition, he reprobated
in the ftrongeft terms every defire of pre-eminence
among his difciples. Yet how little have either
his precepts or his own example been obferved.
We have feen in the church of Rome, with what
eafe the beft fyftem of religion and morals may
be perverted to the moft deteftable purpofes, but

forget

forget, that the fame leaven ferments in the bodies glorying in a feparation from her, and a reformation, as it is improperly called, of her abufes. The love of pre-eminence is the fecond circumftance, that has been a fatal hindrance to the progrefs of chriftianity. The chriftian world has been divided into two parts, clergy and laity, diftinguifhed both by drefs and manners from each other. The clergy every where affect a fuperiority, and in confequence claim to be indulged with peculiar power and privileges. It was natural, that when this pre-eminence was once eftablifhed in the minds of the degraded laity, the clergy fhould get the countenance of the legiflature, for the framing of laws, not only to preferve their own dignity, but to prevent the interference of the people in ecclefiaftical concerns. Hence ecclefiaftical courts, ecclefiaftical ranks and titles, ecclefiaftical drefs, all repugnant to the fpirit of chriftianity. The laity like brute beafts fit tamely under this ufurpation : a man, if a prieft or minifter enters, is not a mafter of his own houfe, he muft not thank god for the bleffings of providence at his own table, he cannot pledge his faith to a lovely woman without the interference of the prieft, his offspring muft be fprinkled by facred hands, and at death he is not committed to his long home without another fpiritual incantation.

Thefe

These superstitious prejudices are without doubt highly beneficial to the interest of the clerical community, but the morals of neither party are consulted. The laity are apt to imagine, that there are some practices, in which they may be indulged without any imputation on their christian character; and the gentleman in black is supposed, to put on a particular set of features and behaviour with his cloaths. The simplicity of the gospel admits nothing of this sort. All christians are equally servants of one common lord, equally bound by his precepts, and equally entitled to the privileges of his religion. It may be necessary to have persons well educated for the instruction of the people and the conducting of the publick worship, but as far as this is regulated by the civil power, the body is political not spiritual. It may be expedient, that one person should conduct the worship of a dissenting congregation, but it is dangerous to associate the performers of this office in a kind of spiritual connection. The dissenters view with an evil eye the visitations of archbishops, bishops, archdeacons etc; but the assemblies of their ministers, whether at the opening of a chapel, the ordaining of a brother minister, or for various other purposes, denote as much love of spiritual pre-eminence, as is to be found in the established church.

It

It would be endlefs to purfue the various evils, that fpring out of this ftrange diftinction among chriftians. Age and abilities command refpect, it is willingly paid by every liberal mind and lover of good order ; from the profeffion alfo of a teacher of chriftianity it ought not to be withheld. But, let it be kept within due bounds, let not the teacher of a petty meeting claim the authority of a pope, let him not be the means of fetting families and congregations at variance. It is a great miftake to fuppofe, that perfecution is confined to eftablifhed churches; there is a pernicious fort prevailing among fectaries, and to diffent from the fociety, of which one is a member, is too frequently attended with the lofs of an income. Not to omit, that the terms heterodox, heretick, deift, infidel are fcattered abroad with great rapidity in diffenting communities, and under pretext of confulting the good of his foul, a narrow-minded congregation will frequently deprive an individual of all his earthly comfort.

The contending parties, whom we are addreffing, will however confider this as a digreffion, and leave to others the care of directing the fpiritual concerns and meliorating the religious opinions of mankind. It fuffices, that we have pointed out fome objects which more immediately call for their attention. Let them endeavour to

remove

remove the tithes, provide for an amendment of
the liturgy, and repeal the teſt act, and having
done this they may ſafely leave farther improvements on a chriſtian baſis to thoſe, who ſhall by
their means be enabled to underſtand better the
principle of true religion.

To every thing, that has been urged in the
preceeding pages, two formidable objections occurr: firſt, that the reforms propoſed are too
numerous, and, ſecondly, that this is by no means
the time to entertain any thoughts of reform.
With reſpect to the number of reforms it may be
anſwered, that we are not to look either to the
number or magnitude but to the expediency of
them, and farther it is not ſuppoſed, that all theſe
reforms ſhould take place at the ſame time: they
are not to be undertaken without due care and
deliberation. Still there are ſome things, which
may be put immediately into execution: the
game and the teſt laws may be repealed, a new
code of criminal law framed, the liturgy reviſed,
and the boroughs regulated in this ſeſſion of parliament. And the people ſeeing, that the houſe
of commons, inſtead of indulging in ſo much
perſonal altercation and frivolous panegyrick, is
ſeriouſly occupied in promoting and improving
the wellfare of the ſtate, will thankfully receive
theſe preſages of better times, and contentedly
wait till a longer period ſhall have put an end to
all their grievances.

The

The trite argument, that this is not the time to reform, can no longer have any weight on the minds of englifhmen. It has been repeated in periods of publick commotion and the profoundeft peace. The natural indolence of man may plead for the fupport of abufes, but the example of a neighbouring nation muft furely produce an effect in the cabinet of every monarch. From neglecting to examine and correct the abufes, prevailing through length of time in an extenfive empire, we have feen a monarch hurled from his throne, the moft powerful nobility in Europe driven from their caftles, and the richeft hierarchy expelled from their altars. Had the monarch feafonably given up fome ufelefs prerogatives, he might ftill have worn the crown ; had the nobility confented to relinquifh thofe feudal privileges, which were defigned only for barbarous ages, they might have retained their titles; could the clergy have fubmitted to be citizens, they might ftill have been in poffeffion of wealth and influence. The proper time to correct any abufe, and remedy any grievance, is the inftant, they are known; if neglected they continue to increafe, till the ruling powers are in fear for their own fafety, and being overawed by the party, interefted in corruption, they can neither retreat nor proceed without endangering the common weal.

Happily

Happily for this country we are in a very different situation. There is no party to overawe the government, and the people are united to give its measures effectual support. Nothing can be forced upon it: every reform must proceed from, and be under the direction of the ruling powers. How much then is it to be desired, that such an opportunity of setting government on its best foundation should not be lost, and that a timely removal of every grievance may render the name of another revolution disgustfull to englishmen. Should this opportunity be lost, it may never occurr again. The discontented party, for there is, we have been informed by high authority, one sufficiently numerous to excite alarm, may increase and by dwelling upon real evils undermine that power, which was resolved not to listen to any terms of reconciliation. Whatever may be our fate with respect to foreign nations, peace and union are the greatest objects at home.

Let the republicans be moderate in their demands, the anti-republicans not pertinacious in opposing every reform, and government, strengthened by the accession of both parties to it as a centre of union, will present to the world a compact body, firmly united to preserve an improving constitution, and to promote the publick happiness.

F I N I ·

APPENDIX,

On the Execution of Louis Capet.

———————

LOUIS CAPET has afforded an excellent topick for parliamentary declamation. Let us ftrip the fubject of figures of rhetorick, and no englifhman need be alarmed at the execution of an individual at Paris. Louis Capet was once king of France, and entitled to the honours due to that exalted ftation. The fupreme power in the nation declared, that France fhould be a republick. from that moment Louis Capet loft his titles. He was accufed of enormous crimes, confined as a ftate prifoner, tried by the national convention, found guilty, condemned, and executed. What is there wonderful in all this? Our revolution, the boaft of the prefent days, purfued the fame conduct as nearly as poffible. Our convention declared, that James the 2d. fhould be no longer king: it did not chufe to abolifh kingfhip, but dignified William the 3d. with regal honours. James was ftripped of his titles, and became plain James Stuart, and the republican William became a fovereign. James was not tried, condemned, executed, becaufe he faved his life by flight: but the laws againft himfelf and his fon, and the proceedings in the years fifteen and forty five muft convince the moft fuperficial reafoner, that the maxims of the englifh

H   and

and french nations, with refpect to the dethron-
ing of kings, are exactly the fame. But fome one
will fay, Louis Capet was unjuftly condemned.
Ninety-nine out of a hundred, who make this objection, have not given themfelves the trouble of
examining the records of the trial : and why
fhould I give greater credit to the remaining ob-
jectour than to the verdict of the court ? If Louis
Capet did, when king, encourage the invafion of
his country, however we may be inclined to pity
the unfortunate man for the errour of his conduct,
we have no right to proclaim him innocent in
point of law. It is in fhort no bufinefs of ours,
and if all the crowned heads on the continent are
taken off, it is no bufinefs of ours. We fhould
be unworthy of the conftitution fettled at the
revolution, and enemies to the Brunfwick family
now feated on our throne, if we denied to any
nation the right of fettling, as it pleafed, its own
internal government. Thefe fentiments do not
prevent us from commiferating the fituation of
the french refugees. They are entitled to our
compaffion : and it is but right, that we fhould
attend to their diftreffes, fince foreign countries
have been put to the expence of maintaining
thofe refugees from our own ifland, who, for their
attachment to an ancient family were, by the ri-
gour of the two foreign reigns, fubjected to all
the penalties exacted from recufants by the prefent government in France.

The Effect of War on the Poor.

THREE days after the debate on the king's message, I was walking from my friend's house to the neighbouring town to inspect the printing of these few sheets, and in my way joined company with two men of the village, who, being employed by the woolstaplers to let out spinning to the poor, had lately received orders to lower the value of labour. We were talking on this subject, when the exclamations of a groupe of poor women going to market overhearing our conversation made an impression on my mind, which all the eloquence of the houses of lords and commons cannot efface. We are to be sconced three-pence in the shilling, let others work for me, I'll not. We are to be sconced a fourth part of our labour. What is all this for? I did not dare to tell them what it was for, nor to add insult to misery. What is the beheading of a monarch to them? What is the navigation of the Scheldt to them? What is the freedom of a great nation to them but reason for joy? Yet the debating only on these subjects has reached their cottages. They are already sconced three pence in the shilling. What must be their fate, when we suffer under the most odious scourge of the human race, and the accumulation of taxes takes

away

away half of that daily bread, which is scarce
sufficient at present for their support?

Oh! that I had the warning voice of an antient prophet, that I might penetrate into the inmost
recesses of palaces, and appall the haranguers of
senates. I would use no other language than
that of the poor market women. I would cry
aloud in the ears of the first magistrate, we are
sconced three-pence in the shilling, the fourth
part of our labour, for what? I would address
myself to the deliberating bodies: we are sconced
three-pence in the shilling, the fourth part of our
labours, for what? Is there a man, that could
stand out against this eloquence? Yes. Thou-
sands. Three-pence in the shilling for spinning
conveys no ideas to them. They know not
what a cottage is, they know not how the poor
live, how they make up their scanty meal. Perhaps there may be some one in our house of commons, whose feelings are in union with mine;
communicate them to your colleagues, impress
them with the horrour attendant on their deliberations, tell them what the deduction of three-
pence in the shilling occasions among the my-
riads of England. And should any grave courtier
pitying the distresses of the poor be anxious to
relieve them, say to him; there is an easy me-
thod: let the first magistrate, the peers, the re-
presentatives of the people, the rich men of the

nation, all who are for war, be sconced one fourth part of their annual income to defray the expence of it. Let them be the first sufferers, let the burden fall on them, not on the poor, Alafs! my poor countrymen, how many years calamity awaits you before a single dish or a glafs of wine will be withdrawn from the tables of opulence.

At this moment perhaps the decree is gone forth for war. Let others talk of glory, let others celebrate the heroes, who are to deluge the world with blood, the words of the poor market women will still refound in my ears, we are sconced three-pence in the shilling, one fourth of our labour. For what!

F I N I S.